Acknowledgements

Beyond the Grill, A Cookbook For Men is dedicated to my husband, Kelly, and my family, all of whom have been so supportive during the writing of this book.
Deuteronomy 8:3

Debbye Dabbs

ISBN: 0-9645899-3-1

Manufactured by
Favorite Recipes® Press
an imprint of

FRP

P.O. Box 305142
Nashville, Tennessee 37230
800-358-0560

TAKE FIVE COOKBOOKS

1583 East County Line Rd., Suite G
Jackson, Mississippi 39211

___ Beyond the Grill, A Cookbook For Men

___ Light Take Five, A Cookbook

___ Take Five, A Cookbook

___ Take Five, A Christmas Cookbook

Please send me ____ copies at $12.00 per copy. I am enclosing $2.00 for postage. (Mississippi residents please add 84 cents tax per book.)

Name_____

Address _____

City _____ State_____ Zip _____

_____ ✛⟶❧ ❧⟵✛ _____

Index

Index

Johnston Family Biscuits

1/2 cup shortening
2 cups self-rising flour
3/4 cup milk

Cut shortening into flour until crumbly. Stir in milk. Form a ball with the dough. Place dough ball on a floured surface. Roll dough one-half inch thick. Cut with cookie cutter and place on cookie sheet. Bake at 450 degrees for 13 minutes.
Yield: 10 biscuits

Broccoli Soup

1 (10-ounce) package frozen chopped broccoli, thawed
3 cans cream of chicken soup
1 (8-ounce) cheddar cheese, grated
$1/2$ teaspoon cayenne pepper
3 cups chicken broth

Heat over low heat until warm.
Yield: 4 servings

Tropical Pineapple Dip

1 (8-ounce) package cream cheese, softened
1 (8-ounce) can crushed pineapple, drained
1 tablespoon finely diced onion
$1/2$ teaspoon garlic salt

Beat cream cheese until fluffy. Add pineapple, onion and garlic salt.
Chill. Serve with crackers.
Yield: 8 servings

Pizza Ryes

1 pound of hot sausage
1 pound of Velveeta cheese
1 tablespoon worcestershire sauce
$\frac{1}{4}$ to $\frac{1}{2}$ teaspoon garlic powder
4 loaves party rye bread

Cook meat only until it loses its pink color. Drain. Add Velveeta cheese cut into cubes. Melt on lowered heat. Add worcestershire and garlic powder. Mix and let cool. Spread with a spoon onto bread. Bake at 375 degrees for 10 to 15 minutes.
Yield: 25 pizzas

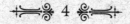

Shrimp Sandwiches

2 (3-ounce) packages of cream cheese
2 (5-ounce) cans shrimp
1 cup mayonnaise
2 teaspoons grated onion
1 tablespoon worcestershire sauce

Mix all ingredients well in blender. Chill and spread on bread for sandwiches.
Yield: 8 sandwiches

Mint Cooler

1 cup water
$^1/_2$ cup sugar
$^1/_4$ cup chopped mint or $^1/_2$ teaspoon mint flavor
$^1/_2$ cup lemon juice
1 quart or liter bottle chilled ginger ale

Combine water, sugar and mint in saucepan. Bring to boil stirring constantly until sugar dissolves. Remove from heat. Strain mint and discard. Stir in lemon juice. Chill. Add ginger ale and serve over crushed ice.
Yield: 6 (8-ounce) cups

Tailgate Cheese Dip

2 (8-ounce) packages cream cheese
1 pound sausage, cooked and drained
1 (10-ounce) can Rotel tomatoes

Combine all ingredients. Heat in microwave for 3 minutes and stir.
Repeat until warm. Serve with chips.
Yield: 4 cups

Pea Soup Shelton

1 1/2 pounds dry split peas
1 to 1 1/2 cups diced ham
1 medium onion, finely diced
2 to 3 carrots, diced
2 teaspoons salt

Wash peas. Place peas, ham, onions, carrots and seasonings in a pot with 3 quarts of water. Bring to a boil, stirring occasionally. Cover and let simmer 1 1/2 hours. Stir occasionally. Can be frozen.
Yield: 10 to 12 servings

Lemonade Tea

4 cups boiling water
6 tea bags
1 (6-ounce) can frozen lemonade
1½ cups sugar
12 cups water

Pour boiling water over tea bags and let set 10 minutes. In a large
container mix next 4 ingredients. Add tea and chill. Keep refrigerated.
Yield: 1 gallon

Spinach Dip

1 (10-ounce) package chopped spinach
1 cup mayonnaise
1 cup sour cream
1 (8-ounce) can water chestnuts, minced
1 envelope Knorr's dry vegetable soup mix

Thaw spinach. Press all water out of the spinach. Add remaining ingredients and mix well. Refrigerate 2 hours before serving.
Yield: 16 ounces

Best Onion Soup

5 large onions, thinly sliced
$1/4$ cup butter
4 ($10^1/2$-ounce) cans beef broth
$1^1/2$ cups water
French bread, thinly sliced

Sauté onions in butter for 15 minutes. Add beef broth to onions and butter. Add water and simmer for 1 hour or longer. Put soup into ramekin or small cup. Place slice of French bread on top of serving. Brown under the broiler.
Yield: 8 (6-ounce) servings

Harris Ham Sandwiches

1 cup margarine
2 teaspoons Creole mustard
24 small sesame seed rolls
1 (12-ounce) package sliced ham
8 ounces Monterey Jack cheese

Melt margarine. Mix margarine and mustard. Remove tops of rolls with an electric knife. Spread tops and bottoms of rolls with margarine mixture. Place ham and cheese on each roll. Replace top. Wrap tightly in foil. Bake at 350 degrees for 30 minutes.
Yield: 24 sandwiches

Louys Lime Punch

1 pint lime sherbet, softened
1 small can frozen lemonade
1 (2-liter) bottle ginger ale, chilled

Mix and serve in a large punch bowl.
Yield: 10 servings

West Texas Cheese Spread

1 (16-ounce) package colby cheese, shredded
1 (4-ounce) jar pimento, drained and chopped
1 cup mayonnaise
10 green olives, chopped
3/4 teaspoon lemon pepper

Mix and spread on thin sliced bread.
Yield: 6 sandwiches

Artichoke Spinach Dip

2 jars marinated artichoke hearts, drained and diced
1 (10-ounce) package chopped spinach, thawed and drained
1/2 cup sour cream
1/2 cup mayonnaise
1 cup shredded fresh parmesan

Mix together and heat at 350 degrees for 10 minutes until hot. Serve with crackers.
Yield: 8 servings

McDade Cheese Muffins

1 (16-ounce) package sausage, cooked
1 (11-ounce) can cheese soup
1/2 cup water
3 cups biscuit mix

Mix together in a large bowl. Put in greased mini muffin tins and bake at 400 degrees for 15 minutes.
Yield: 36 servings

Wild Rice Casserole

1/2 pound fresh mushrooms, sliced
1/2 cup butter or margarine
2 tablespoons flour
1 cup milk
1 (6-ounce) box long grain and wild rice, cooked according to
   package directions

Sauté mushrooms in butter or margarine. Add flour and blend
well. Add milk and cook on medium heat, stirring until mixture
has thickened. Add cooked rice and blend well.
Yield: 4 to 6 servings

Spinach-Artichoke Casserole

2 (3-ounce) packages cream cheese
2 ounces bleu cheese
$1/2$ cup butter
2 (10-ounce) packages frozen chopped spinach
1 ($13^3/4$-ounce) can artichoke hearts, drained

In a small saucepan, cook cream cheese, bleu cheese and butter over low heat. Cook spinach. Drain well. Combine spinach with cream cheese mixture. In a greased $1^1/2$-quart casserole, arrange artichoke hearts and pour spinach mixture over them. Cook at 350 degrees for 20 minutes. Yield: 4 servings

Heavenly Hash Brown Casserole

1 (32-ounce) package frozen shredded potatoes, thawed
1 (10$\frac{1}{2}$-ounce) can cream of chicken soup, undiluted
12 ounces cheddar cheese, shredded
1 (8-ounce) carton sour cream
$\frac{1}{2}$ small onion, chopped

Place potatoes in a 9x13-inch casserole dish. Mix together the next
4 ingredients and pour over potatoes. Bake, uncovered at 350 degrees
for 45 minutes. Freezes well.
Yield: 12 servings

Ed's Barley Bake

6 tablespoons butter
2/3 cup onion
2 cups medium pearled barley, rinsed and drained
6 cups water
6 chicken-flavored bouillon cubes, crumbled

Heat oven to 325 degrees. In a heavy skillet melt butter over medium heat. Stir in onion and barley. Cook 5 minutes or until barley is lightly browned. Add water and bouillon cubes. Bring to a boil. Pour into covered casserole and bake 1 hour and 15 minutes.
Yield: 8 servings

Oven-Roasted Sweet Potatoes and Onions

4 medium peeled sweet potatoes, cut into 2-inch pieces
    (about 2^1/$_2$ pounds)
2 medium Vidalia or other sweet onion, sliced
2 tablespoons extra-virgin olive oil
^{3}/$_4$ teaspoon garlic-pepper blend
^{1}/$_2$ teaspoon salt

Preheat oven to 425 degrees. Combine all ingredients in a 9x13-inch baking dish, tossing to coat. Bake at 425 degrees for 35 minutes or until tender, stirring occasionally.
Yield: 6 servings

Green Bean Bundles

8 uncooked bacon strips, cut into halves
1 can whole green beans
1 bottle French salad dressing
16 toothpicks

Wrap 4 or 5 green beans with 1/2 bacon strip. Secure with a toothpick.
Place in a 9x13-inch baking dish. Cover with dressing and bake at
350 degrees for 30 minutes.
Yield: 8 servings

Spinach Robinson

2 (10-ounce) packages frozen spinach, cooked and drained
1 (8-ounce) container French onion dip
1 teaspoon garlic salt
1 teaspoon worcestershire sauce
1 (6-ounce) roll jalapeño cheese, melted

Mix together and place in greased casserole. Bake at 350 degrees for
15 minutes.
Yield: 6 servings

Corn à la McCart

2 cans cream style corn
1 box Jiffy cornbread mix
1/2 cup oil
3 eggs, beaten
1 (8-ounce) carton sour cream

Mix ingredients. Pour into an 8x8 greased baking dish. Bake at
350 degrees for 30 minutes.
Yield: 8 servings

Morgan Red Beans

1 medium onion, chopped
1 medium bell pepper, chopped
1 pound medium sausage
2 (10-ounce) cans diced mild tomatoes and green chilies
2 cans red beans, do not drain

Brown onion, peppers and sausage in a large skillet. Add remaining ingredients and simmer for 1 hour over low heat. Serve over rice. Yield: 6 servings

Cranberry Salad

1 (3-ounce) package cherry gelatin
1 cup hot water
1 (16-ounce) can whole cranberry sauce
1/2 cup chopped pecans
1 (8-ounce) carton sour cream

Dissolve gelatin in water. Break up cranberry sauce with fork, then add to gelatin. Add pecans. Fold in sour cream and put mixture into 1 quart mold. Chill.
Yield: 8 servings

German Potato Salad

16 unpeeled new potatoes, cooked and sliced
1/4 cup chopped onion
1/3 cup sweet pickle relish
1/2 cup mayonnaise
3 tablespoons mustard

Mix in large bowl. Cover and chill.
Yield: 8 servings

Raspberry Spinach Salad

1 package fresh spinach
1 small box fresh mushrooms, sliced
$1/2$ cup bacon bits
$1/2$ cup raspberry jam
1 bottle Italian salad dressing

Toss spinach, mushrooms and bacon bits. Warm jam and dressing in microwave for about 30 seconds. Pour over salad and serve.
Yield: 4 servings

Segrest Salad

1 large head romaine lettuce
1 small bag frozen English peas, thawed
2 cups grated cheddar cheese
1 cup real bacon bits
1 small bottle peppercorn ranch salad dressing

Wash lettuce and drain. Tear into small pieces. Toss with peas, cheese and bacon bits. Top with dressing and toss before serving.
Yield: 6 servings

Shell Pasta Salad

3 cups (8-ounces) uncooked shell pasta
1 cup frozen broccoli cuts
1 (8-ounce) bottle ranch salad dressing
1 (10-ounce) can chicken chunks, drained
3 ounces fresh parmesan cheese, grated

Cook pasta as directed on package. Add broccoli during the last
2 minutes of cooking time. Drain well. In a large bowl, toss pasta
and remaining ingredients. Refrigerate 2 hours.
Yield: 6 servings

Shrimp Salad

3 pounds shrimp, cooked and peeled
2 hard-cooked eggs, chopped
$1/2$ cup sweet pickle relish
$1/4$ cup sweet onion, chopped
$1^1/2$ cups mayonnaise

Combine first 4 ingredients in a large bowl. Add mayonnaise and toss.
Cover and chill.
Yield: 6 servings

Derby Day Salad

1 head lettuce, shredded
3 hard-cooked eggs, chopped
6 slices crisp bacon, crumbled
¾ cup crumbled Roquefort cheese
2 medium avocados, peeled and sliced

Place lettuce in large salad bowl. Arrange eggs, bacon and cheese on top. Garnish with avocado slices. Toss before serving.
Yield: 8 servings

Grilled Salmon Steaks

1/2 cup olive oil
1/2 cup cooking wine
1/2 cup soy sauce
2 cloves garlic, minced
4 (6 to 8-ounce) salmon steaks

Mix first 4 ingredients in small bowl. Place steaks in a small baking dish. Cover with marinade and chill for 2 hours. Drain and grill over medium coals about ten minutes.
Yield: 4 servings

Hataway Chicken Surprise

1 whole fryer
1 can cola, opened
1/2 cup olive oil
2 teaspoons salt

Clean and wash chicken. Remove giblets from cavity. Place chicken cavity over can of opened cola. Brush with 1/4 cup oil and 1 teaspoon salt. Place on gas or electic grill. Cook covered for 1 hour. (Brush with remaining oil and salt after 30 minutes.)
Yield: 3 servings

Trent's Steak Marinade

1 small bottle Italian salad dressing
1/2 cup worcestershire sauce
1 lemon
1/2 cup steak sauce
4 ribeye steaks

Mix first 4 ingredients together. Place steaks and marinade in a large zip-lock bag. Chill for 2 hours before grilling. Drain and grill on moderate heat.
Yield: 4 servings

Bubba's Burgers

1 envelope onion soup mix
$1/2$ cup water
2 pounds ground beef

In large bowl, combine all ingredients. Shape into 8 patties. Grill or broil until done.
Yield: 8 servings

Chicken "Beyond Good"

3 tablespoons butter (not margarine)
2 tablespoons flour
4 tablespoons heavy cream
1 tablespoon creamed horseradish sauce
4 chicken breast filets, grilled

Melt butter in skillet. Slowly stir in flour, cream and horseradish sauce.
Spoon sauce over each grilled chicken breast.
Yield: 4 servings

Easy Chicken Melts

4 ($\frac{1}{2}$-inch thick) onion slices
4 ($\frac{1}{2}$-inch thick) red bell pepper rings
4 boneless, skinless chicken breast halves
1 cup shredded colby-Monterey Jack cheese blend
4 large kaiser rolls, split

Place onion, bell pepper and chicken on grill over medium-high heat. Cook vegetables 1$\frac{1}{2}$ to 2 minutes. Remove from grill. Cook chicken 5 to 7 minutes on each side. During last 2 minutes of cooking, sprinkle cheese on chicken. When cheese is melted, place chicken on kaiser rolls and top each with grilled vegetables.
Yield: 4 servings

Martens Tenderloin Marinade

2¾ pounds pork tenderloin
1 cup soy sauce
4 teaspoons butter, melted
¼ cup white wine
½ cup orange juice

Place all ingredients in a large zip-top plastic bag for 8 hours or overnight. Remove from marinade and grill over medium coals for 12 minutes on each side.
Yield: 6 servings

Chicken on the Grill

¹/₂ cup soy sauce
¹/₄ cup brown sugar
1 teaspoon ground ginger
1 tablespoon cooking oil
4 chicken breast, deboned

Mix first 4 ingredients. Pour mixture over chicken breasts and marinate overnight. Grill over low-heat coals for 45 minutes.
Yield: 4 servings

Kelly's Chili

1 pound ground beef
1 package chili seasoning mix
2 (8-ounce) cans tomato sauce
1 (16-ounce) can kidney beans
1½ cups water

Brown meat and drain. Add remaining ingredients. Cover and simmer
for 1 hour. Stir often.
Yield: 6 servings

Cajun Eggs

4 green onions, finely chopped
$1/4$ cup butter
$1/2$ cup chopped ham
8 eggs, well beaten
$1/4$ cup milk or cream

Sauté onions in butter. Add chopped ham and then beaten eggs mixed with milk or cream. Stir slowly until done but still moist. Season to taste.
Yield: 4 to 6 servings

Rick's Italian Spice Chicken

4 chicken breasts, cubed and cooked
$1/2$ bag chopped frozen red, green pepper and onion mix
2 medium zucchini cubed
$1/2$ teaspoon Italian seasoning
2 cloves garlic, chopped and pressed

Saute onion, peppers and zucchini just until crispy tender. Add Italian seasoning and garlic. Add cooked chicken to vegetables and cook until heated thoroughly. Serve over rice or angel hair pasta.
Yield: 4 servings

Barbecued Brisket

1 (5-ounce) bottle liquid smoke
1 (14-ounce) bottle ketchup
2 cups brown sugar
2 tablespoons dry mustard
1 (2 to 3 pound) brisket, with fat

Mix liquid smoke, ketchup, brown sugar and mustard. Place brisket in a 9x13-inch casserole, fat side up. Pour mixture over brisket. Bake at 250 degrees for 5 hours, uncovered.
Yield: 8 servings

Chicken Saint Petersburg

1/4 cup corn oil
1 (8-ounce) bottle Russian salad dressing
1 envelope dry onion soup mix
1 (10-ounce) jar apricot preserves
8 chicken breasts

Mix together all ingredients except chicken. Place chicken in single layer, skin-side up, in large shallow baking pan. Pour preserves mixture on chicken. Bake covered in 350 degree oven for 1 1/2 hours.
Yield: 8 servings

Sea Scape Casserole

1 pound fresh lump crabmeat
4 ounces cream cheese, cubed
4 ounces shredded cheddar cheese
¼ cup milk
2 ounces sherry

Mix all ingredients and put into a 2-quart glass casserole dish. Bake at
350 degrees for about 35 minutes.
Yield: 4 to 6 servings

T. J.'s Pizza

1 (10-ounce) thin, baked pizza crust
1 (6-ounce) roll jalapeño pepper cheese
1 can guacamole dip
1 small box frozen spinach, cooked and drained
2 cups shredded mozzarella cheese

Place crust on greased baking sheet. Mix next 3 ingredients and place in a small saucepan. Heat for 3 minutes. Spoon mixture over crust. Top with grated cheese. Bake at 350 degrees for 15 minutes.
Yield: 4 servings

Summer Chicken Salad

4 cups cooked and chunked chicken breast
1 small can crushed pineapple, drained
1 cup finely chopped celery
1½ cups seedless grapes, halved
½ cup mayonnaise

Combine chicken with remaining ingredients.
Yield: 4 servings

Sonny's Pork Tenderloin

2¾ pounds pork tenderloin
½ cup soy sauce
2 teaspoons ginger
¼ cup white wine
½ cup orange juice

Place all ingredients in a large zip-top plastic bag for 8 hours or overnight. Remove from marinade and bake on a broiler pan at 350 degrees for 55 minutes.
Yield: 6 servings

Brad's Roast

1 oven bag, small size
3 tablespoons flour
1 envelope onion soup mix
2 tablespoons vinegar
1 (3-pound) pot roast or rump roast

Shake flour in bag. Add soup and vinegar to bag. Add roast and place in baking dish. Cut 6 slits in top of bag and bake at 275 degrees for 4 hours.
Yield: 6 servings

Shrimp Creole

2 tablespoons cooking oil
2 cups chopped frozen onion and bell pepper mix
1 (16-ounce) tomato sauce
1 teaspoon red pepper
2 pounds raw shrimp, peeled

Sauté onion mix in oil. Add tomato sauce, seasoning and shrimp. Cook slowly for 1 hour. Serve with rice.
Yield: 6 servings

"Honey Do" Chicken

4 boneless, skinless chicken breast
4 ounces butter
6 tablespoons honey
4 tablespoons chopped walnuts
2 lemons

In a sauté pan, heat butter over medium-high heat and sauté chicken breasts for approximately 2 minutes per side. Chicken should be cooked, but not dry. Top with honey and walnuts. Squeeze juice from both lemons over top of chicken before serving.
Yield: 4 servings

Joe Morris Beans

3 (15-ounce) cans pinto beans
1 cup chopped onion
1 cup chopped bell pepper
$1/2$ envelope chili seasoning mix
1 pound summer sausage, cut into 1 inch pieces

Mix and cook over low heat for 2 hours. Serve over rice.
Yield: 6 servings

Chicken and Friends

1 large bell pepper, sliced
2 large potatoes, sliced
4 chicken breasts, deboned
2 small onions, sliced
2 cans cream of chicken soup

Place first 4 ingredients in a greased casserole dish. Top with soup.
Cover with foil and bake at 350 degrees for 1 hour.
Yield: 4 servings

Main Event

Rigatoni with Mushrooms

1 pound rigatoni, cooked and drained
2 cups sliced fresh mushrooms
2 cans tomatoes and green chilies, undrained
1 cup ricotta cheese
2 cups shredded mozzarella cheese

Place cooked rigatoni in a greased 9x13-inch baking dish. Cover with mushrooms and tomatoes and chilies. Top with ricotta and mozzarella cheeses. Cover and bake for 20 minutes at 350 degrees.
Yield: 6 servings

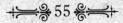

Gibb's Cashew Chicken

1/2 cup butter
1 large onion, sliced
4 boneless chicken breasts, cooked and cubed
1 cup cashew nuts
2 cans cream of chicken soup

Brown onion in butter. Add cashews, chicken and soup. Simmer for 10 minutes. Serve over cooked rice.
Yield: 4 servings

A "Majure" Shrimp Boil

3 pounds shrimp, in the shell
6 lemons, cut in halves
1 stick butter, melted
1/2 cup chili sauce
1 large bottle Italian salad dressing

Place shrimp in covered casserole. Squeeze lemon over shrimp. Cover
with remaining ingredients. Bake covered at 400 degrees for 1 hour.
Yield: 6 servings

Jim's Baked Quail

4 tablespoons brown sugar
1 cup salad oil
1 cup white cooking wine
1/2 cup teriyaki sauce
10 quail

Combine first 4 ingredients. Pour over quail and marinate for 2 hours.
Remove from marinade and bake at 325 degrees for 1 hour.
Yield: 10 servings

Dorsey's Enchilada Bake

2 cans cream of chicken soup
1 can diced tomatoes and green chilies
2 (10-ounce) cans chicken, do not drain
2 cups sharp cheese, grated
8 flour tortilla shells

Mix first 4 ingredients in a large bowl. Fill each shell with 1/2 cup of mixture. Roll and place in 9x13-inch casserole. Cover with remaining mixture and bake at 350 degrees for 30 minutes.
Yield: 4 servings

Shrimp Ladner

1 pound medium shrimp, peeled
2 tablespoons flour
3 tablespoons butter, unsalted
1/3 cup cooking wine
2 teaspoons garlic salt

Dip shrimp in flour and set aside. Melt butter in heavy skillet. Sauté shrimp in butter on medium heat until pink. Add remaining ingredients. Stir until thickened. Serve over steamed rice.
Yield: 4 servings

Guckert Favorite

1 stick butter
1 can diced tomatoes and green chilies
2 cans cream of mushroom soup
1 cup raw rice
2 cups peeled shrimp or chopped chicken

Melt butter in a 9x13-inch casserole dish. Add remaining ingredients.
Bake uncovered at 350 degrees for 45 minutes.
Yield: 6 servings

Blueberry Crispy Pie

3 cups fresh or frozen blueberries
1 cup sugar
1 large can crushed pineapple
1 yellow cake mix
1 stick margarine, melted

Mix first 3 ingredients. Place in a greased 9x13-inch baking dish. Sprinkle cake mix over fruit. Top with melted margarine. Bake at 350 degrees for 35 minutes.
Yield: 8 servings

E-Z Banana Pudding

6 bananas
1 box vanilla wafers
2 (3 1/2-ounce) packages instant vanilla pudding
3 cups milk
1 (12-ounce) frozen non-dairy whipped topping

Layer bananas and vanilla wafers in a large bowl. Mix milk, pudding and whipped topping. Pour over bananas and vanilla wafers.
Yield: 8 servings

Chocolate Chess Pie

1/2 stick margarine
3 tablespoons cocoa powder
1 1/2 cups sugar
2 eggs
3/4 cup evaporated milk

Melt butter and stir in cocoa. Add sugar and mix well. Add eggs, one at a time. Gradually stir in evaporated milk. Pour filling into unbaked pie shell and bake at 325 degrees for 40 to 45 minutes.
Yield: 6 servings

Cocoon Cookies

1 cup butter
4 tablespoons powdered sugar
2 cups flour
1 cup chopped nuts
1 teaspoon vanilla

Cream butter. Stir in sugar and flour. Add nuts and vanilla. Roll heaping teaspoon with hand into small cocoon shape. Bake at 300 degrees for 45 minutes.
Yield: 2 dozen cookies

Dad's Cheesecake

2 (8-ounce) packages cream cheese, softened
¾ cup sugar
1 teaspoon vanilla
2 eggs, beaten
1 graham cracker crust (9-inch)

Mix cream cheese, sugar and vanilla with mixer on medium speed. Add eggs. Pour into crust. Bake 350 degrees for 40 minutes.
Yield: 10 servings

Ice Cream Cake

1 large angel food cake
1 (18-ounce) jar chocolate fudge sauce
1 gallon vanilla ice cream, softened
1/2 pint heavy cream, whipped
Slivered chocolate (optional)

Tear cake into large pieces. Stir in chocolate sauce and coat pieces of cake. Mix in softened ice cream. Put into angel food cake pan and freeze 3 to 4 hours. Turn out onto large cake plate and frost with whipped cream. Decorate with slivered chocolate or as desired. Refreeze.
Yield: 20 servings

Whipping Cream Pound Cake

3 cups sugar
1 cup butter (no substitute)
6 eggs
3 cups cake flour
1/2 pint heavy cream

Grease and flour a bundt cake pan. In large bowl, cream sugar and butter. Add eggs and flour alternately, mixing well. Add cream. Beat at low speed until smooth. Put in cold oven. Bake 1 hour and 25 minutes at 325 degrees.
Yield: 12 servings

Grobe Ice Cream Pie

1 prepared chocolate cookie crust
1 quart vanilla ice cream
1 package Heath Bar Bits

Soften ice cream. Mix with Heath Bar Bits, saving a few to sprinkle on top. Pile into cookie crust. Top with saved Heath Bar Bits. Freeze.
Yield: 6 to 8 servings

Lemon Lotus Ice Cream

1 cup fresh lemon juice
3 cups sugar
2 teaspoons almond extract
2 quarts half and half

Mix lemon juice and sugar. Chill overnight. Add almond extract and half and half to lemon mixture. Freeze according to ice cream freezer directions.
Yield: 8 servings

Sporty's Grape Crush

3 cups sugar
1 pint 100 percent grape juice
1 (8¼-ounce) can crushed pineapple
2 pints whipping cream
3 cups milk

Mix sugar, grape juice and pineapple. Chill for 8 hours or overnight.
Pour all ingredients into ice cream freezer. Freeze as directed.
Yield: 6 servings

Happy Endings

Peanut Butter Pie

1 (8-ounce) package cream cheese
$1/2$ cup peanut butter
1 can sweetened condensed milk
1 (8-ounce) container non-dairy whipped topping
1 ready-to-use chocolate cookie crust

Mix first 3 ingredients with hand mixer until creamy. Fold in non-dairy topping. Pour into pie shell. Refrigerate for 3 hours.
Yield: 8 servings

Peaches au Gratin

1 large can peach halves, drained
4 tablespoons butter, melted
4 tablespoons sugar
12 macaroons, crumbled
1 cup lemon yogurt

Place peaches in baking dish, cut side up. Cover with butter, sugar and macaroom crumbs. Bake at 350 degrees for 30 minutes. Top with lemon yogurt and serve.
Yield: 8 servings

Robert's "Big Orange" Sherbet

1 can sweetened condensed milk
1 small can crushed pineapple, do not drain
6 (12-ounce) cans orange soft drink

Pour into ice cream freezer and freeze as directed.
Yield: 6 servings

Blue Ribbon Brownies

1 (21-ounce) brownie mix
1 egg
1 (8-ounce) container strawberry yogurt
1 cup mini-marshmallows
1 can chocolate frosting

Mix first 3 ingredients in a small bowl about 40 strokes. Spread into a greased 9x13-inch baking pan. Bake at 350 degrees for 25 minutes. While brownies are hot, spread marshmallows on top. Cool and frost with chocolate frosting.

Yield: 10 servings

Tom's Bananas Foster

1 package 9-inch ready-to-use crepes
$^1/_3$ cup butter
5 to 6 bananas, sliced
$^1/_2$ cup maple syrup
whipped cream or ice cream

In a large skillet, melt butter and add bananas. Cook for 4 minutes on medium heat. Add syrup and cook for 2 more minutes on medium low heat. Divide banana mixture between crepes. Roll up crepes and serve topped with whipped cream or ice cream.
Yield: 6 servings